Ghostly Tales of Michigan

by

Ryan Jacobson

Adventure Publications, Inc.
Cambridge, Minnesota

Dedication:
For Emilie, my "go to" girl for all things scary. And for Dana and Tonya, who tell such frightfully fun tales. (Oinkpew!)

A special thank you to everyone who willingly shared their ghost stories and who allowed me to put their tales into this collection. I appreciate your time and your patience. I would also like to thank the many people who gave me guidance and who pointed me in the right direction during the process of researching this book.

In some instances, names and locations have been changed at the request of sources.

Book and cover design by Jonathan Norberg

Edited by Brett Ortler

Ghostly Tales of Michigan

Table of Contents

GREAT LAKE GHOSTS

Preface

This chilling collection was put together through countless hours of research, interviews and fact-checking. It includes many of Michigan's most famous haunts, some of the state's more obscure ghost stories and even a few terrifying tales that have never before been recorded.

The narratives were written using the information gathered, but some of the details were provided to me as checklists of unexplainable occurrences rather than *Ghostly Tales*. Therefore, while the information remains accurate, some of the scenarios (and characters) were reinterpreted for dramatic effect.

I can neither verify the validity of each claim nor the existence of supernatural beings, but I can assure you that the portrayals of the spirits in this book are as accurate as possible.

Enjoy!

Haunted Homes

Poltergeist

It happened again.

When Victor Lincoln discovered his home's (usually locked) front door hanging wide open, he knew he'd find trouble inside. He stepped into the house, and his fears were confirmed: His family's Jackson, Michigan, house had been broken into and vandalized. Garbage, as well as food from the refrigerator, had been thrown about. Furniture was pushed around and flipped over. Light bulbs were smashed, and the water faucets in the kitchen and in the bathroom were running.

Standing behind Victor, his wife shook her head. "Why are they doing this to us? Even those new double locks won't keep them out!"

"I'll go and call the police again," Victor said, sounding defeated. "Not that it'll do any good."

And so it went for two full years. The Lincolns endured break-in after break-in. Nothing could keep the intruders out of their home, and no one could guess who might be targeting them—or why.

But then, in October of 1961, the family discovered a startling truth: The vandal wasn't a "who." It was a "what"!

"Victor," Mrs. Lincoln screamed. "Victor, come quickly. Please hurry!"

Responding to his wife's frantic cries, Victor raced into the kitchen. He arrived just in time to see a stack of dishes fly out of the cupboard and smash against the wall, one by one, shattering on impact.

The dishes did so, all on their own.

Footsteps in the Basement

Thump.

Thump.

Thump.

Twenty-two-year-old John Lincoln looked up from his book and toward his mother. "Do you hear that?" he asked.

Mrs. Lincoln, sitting on a living room chair across from her son, nodded. "It sounds like someone's coming up the basement stairs."

They turned to look at the door, waiting in dreadful anticipation as the footfalls grew louder. At the top step, the noise ceased for a moment. It was soon followed by a thunderous *knock!*

John and his mother jumped out of their seats. Victor, who had heard the commotion from the next room, rushed past his family members with his shotgun in hand. He grabbed the door and flung it open; no one was standing behind it.

Victor cautiously led his dog downstairs, but his search for an intruder came up empty. The dog, however, seemed to find something. The Lincolns' pet began to whimper softly, and then it darted back up the steps.

Following that frightful encounter, the Lincolns decided it was time to move out.

First Blood

In the weeks that followed, things went from bad to worse. While the house sat for sale, the spirit became more terrifying. Moaning sounds were heard in the basement. Phantom footsteps patrolled the premises. Books were moved and piled in various locations. And, in one instance, Mrs. Lincoln was attacked.

She was completely alone, lying on the living room couch, enjoying a rare moment of peace and quiet. *This is the life,* she thought.

Suddenly, out of the corner of her eye, Mrs. Lincoln noticed a blur of motion. She spied an object flying toward her. Before she could even flinch, a paring knife grazed her leg. As blood slowly formed atop her fresh scrape, the frightened woman mentally noted—with certainty—that the knife had been safely stowed in a kitchen drawer.

Not long thereafter, the holidays arrived. However, the ghost did not welcome the festivities. Two days after the Christmas tree was up and decorated in their living room, the Lincolns watched in horror as lights, ornaments and tinsel were thrown across the room by an invisible force.

"That's it!" exclaimed Mrs. Lincoln. "We're taking this tree down!"

More Witnesses

Word began to spread about the strange happenings within the haunted home, and the Lincolns found themselves with several visitors—each wanting to experience the poltergeist firsthand.

Mr. and Mrs. Gingras, friends of the family, witnessed the house's gas and water inexplicably turning on. The Gingrases also heard a guest outside walking onto the porch and up to the house's front door. When no one knocked or rang the doorbell, the couple peeked through a window and found that not only was no one standing at the door—there were no footprints in the snow either.

Jackson County Police Officer Harry Kellar visited the house as a skeptic. But he, too, was present when the gas and water turned on by themselves.

Investigative reporter Raymond Meagher studied the home most extensively, spending ten hours (over three separate trips) inside the place. Along with four other investigators, Meagher remained in the living room with the entire Lincoln family, waiting for something peculiar to occur.

It took a while, but eventually the bathroom water and the gas seemed to activate automatically, while everyone present was in the living room. The group moved through the house to get a closer look, when they heard the sound of glass shattering.

"It seems that a small bottle was thrown against this closet door," said one of the men. "There are shards of glass everywhere."

Suddenly, as the team examined the strange scene, all of the lights inexplicably turned off!

Despite these bizarre incidents, the investigation yielded no conclusive evidence of a haunting, as each event could have been attributed (however unlikely) to an elaborate hoax.

Moving Out

At last, in the summer of 1962, the Lincoln family sold the house and moved away. By all accounts, the ghostly disturbances ceased as soon as the Lincolns were gone.

The home had been in the Lincoln family for several generations, dating back to 1912. This, coupled with the fact that the haunting grew most intense after the Lincolns decided to move, led some to speculate that the family was terrorized by a deceased relative who was protesting the sale of the property.

Scary Sleepovers

Joanie Ferrell was not a psychic. She did not earn a living as a fortune teller or as a paranormal investigator. In 2006, she was a "typical" working mom and a proud new grandmother in her late forties. However, there was something special about Joanie that she kept a well-guarded secret: She saw ghosts from time to time. When her father died nearly thirty years earlier, Joanie's "inner eye" had been awakened. Thus, she could perceive spirits attached to particular places and objects. But none of the specters were more disturbing than the one she encountered while visiting her grandchild, Joseph, and his parents, Ron and Lucy, in Flint.

Like most other grandparents, Joanie lived for her time shared with Joseph. She took an unpaid day off work every week, driving forty minutes from her home to provide child care for the beloved little boy.

Not surprisingly, winter brought forecasts of severe weather. The night before a predicted blizzard, Joanie packed a bag and drove to Flint ahead of the storm, rather than passing up a day with Joseph (and leaving her daughter in a daycare pinch).

"We don't have a spare bed," Lucy warned her mother. "But Ron can sleep on the couch, and you can sleep in bed with me."

"Don't be ridiculous," Joanie protested. "I'll be just fine on the couch."

And so it was decided. When Joanie arrived shortly before bedtime, the old plaid couch was made up for her. A brief conversation and a few "goodnights" later, Joanie was alone in the living room, nodding off to sleep.

The middle of the night brought a disturbing vision. It was almost like a bad dream—except Joanie was awake (and after thirty years of seeing ghosts, she could easily distinguish a dream from a vision).

She was visited by the spirit of an elderly woman. The ghost appeared as little more than skin and bones. Her white robe was stained and soiled. Her long, gray hair was matted and unkempt.

Joanie immediately understood that the specter had some connection to the couch. Before the elderly woman passed away, she had been placed upon it, and she had been neglected—abandoned by those who were supposed to care for her. She had died a miserable death.

Now, the old woman's soul was angry. She wanted to enact her revenge!

The spirit moved forward, threateningly. Joanie leapt off the couch, but as soon as she did so, the supernatural visitor vanished.

Joanie spent the rest of the night on the floor.

When morning came, she asked her daughter, "Can you remind me where you got that couch?"

"Ron picked it up at a garage sale last summer," said Lucy. "It's not very comfortable, is it?"

Joanie agreed, but she said nothing about her ghostly encounter. She didn't want to alarm her daughter, since she sensed that the ghost—while angry—was harmless.

A few weeks later, Joanie once again found herself spending the night. She decided to give the couch another try, but this time the ghost didn't wait. Even before Joanie fell asleep, the old woman appeared. Joanie could almost taste the woman's hatred and grew certain that the ghost would have attacked if she were able. The end result was another night on the floor.

Joanie never tried sleeping on that couch again. She also kept the ghost a secret from Ron and Lucy, until the following summer when the couch was discarded for a newer, more comfortable piece of furniture.

Upon hearing Joanie's account, Ron was able to recall the neighborhood—but not the exact house—where he had purchased the haunted sofa, although he believed it would not have mattered. He remembered that it had been a very large, multi-family sale.

As for Joanie, she found her sleepovers much more relaxing once the old couch was gone. She did not see the woman's ghost again. Yet she couldn't help but wonder if the sofa—and its angry spirit—ever found its way into another unsuspecting home.

The Lifesaving Specter

Daniel and Cora Shopwell were weary of their farming struggles. They were eager for a fresh start. Fortunately, Cora's parents, George and Delilah Hepner, offered just such an opportunity.

"There's an empty lot across the street from us," Cora's mother explained. "The house that used to stand there burned to the ground years ago. Why don't you come live here, and we'll help you get back on your feet?"

Thus, it was decided. In 1903, the young couple moved to the small village of Lake Odessa. Daniel built their new house atop the stone foundation that stood near Tupper Lake Street and Sixth Avenue.

It seemed like a dream come true for the Shopwells. They had a beautiful place of their own, close to family. Their new life was set to begin. Unfortunately, the happy plans were derailed by an unexpected presence.

Knock. Knock. Knock.

"Who would be visiting at this hour?" Cora asked, about to lie down for the night.

Daniel shrugged. His only guess was Cora's parents.

Knock! Knock! Knock!

The pounding grew louder, sounding more urgent.

Daniel leapt out of bed and hurried to the front door. When he flung it open, he found no one there.

"Who was it?" asked Cora, as Daniel returned to the bedroom.

Her husband shrugged again. "No one, I guess."

Suddenly, behind him, Daniel heard the creak of the front door being opened. It was instantly followed by a loud slam that seemed to shake the entire house.

For a second time, Daniel raced out the bedroom. And once again, he found no one inside (or outside) the house.

The instance was one of several curious happenings. Loud banging noises seemed to emanate from all corners of the home. Windows and doors were frequently rattled by unexplained knocks. Even the sitting room's wood-burning stove acted peculiarly. Its door would swing open and closed, as if an invisible force were checking it. And perhaps strangest of all, the Shopwells sometimes heard a heavy ball rolling across their porch—a ball that could never be found.

Late one night, while Daniel was sitting in the living room, his chair suddenly lifted off the ground. It levitated for several seconds before falling back to the floor.

For the Shopwells, that was the last straw. They sold the property and moved back to their old farm.

A short time later, Gottlieb and Anna Kussmaul moved into the old Shopwell house with their only child, Hattie. The couple were hardworking, enthusiastic, first-generation Americans with a solid reputation within the community. However, the haunted home had plenty of tricks in store for them, too.

At first, the Kussmauls believed all of the knocking, slamming doors and other strange noises were the work of their mischievous daughter. However, that opinion changed when, one day, Hattie ran to a neighbor's house. She was in a hysterical fright.

"I saw a ghost," she cried. "He was in our bathroom. He was shining his boots!" When the child calmed down, she described the scene in further detail. "I could see right through him," Hattie noted. "That's how I knew he was a real ghost."

A subsequent search of the house yielded no evidence that anyone else had been there. But Hattie's conviction, coupled with all of the other strange phenomena, led the girl's parents to believe her.

A few weeks later, neighbors claimed to hear two men violently fighting inside the house. It was such a disturbing ruckus that they contacted the police.

"We can hear them hitting and grunting," said one of the neighbors. "It sounds like they're pounding each other against the floor."

Another search of the home also came up empty. The cause of the noises was never determined.

Eventually, the Kussmauls learned to live with their ghostly guest. The family grew accustomed to the strange sounds and peculiar incidents within the home. The spirit seemed harmless. In fact, it turned out to be quite helpful.

Late one night, Anna bolted upright in bed. She stared, aghast, as the ghost of a man appeared beside her. The gray specter gestured toward Anna's husband.

In that instant, Anna realized something was wrong with Gottlieb. "Wake up!" she shouted, shaking him.

Her husband did not stir.

"Gottlieb!" she screamed, slapping his face.

Still he did not respond.

Unable to rouse him, Anna did the only thing she could: she summoned medical help.

The woman later learned that Gottlieb had a seizure during the night. But fortunately, the doctor arrived in time to revive him. The ghost had likely saved Gottlieb's life.

As stories of this lifesaving specter got out, the Kussmauls became the subject of many interviews and much media exposure. It led some experts to trace the spirit back to a wealthy man who had once lived on the property. Rumors circulated that he was robbed and then murdered in his home, which was later torched to destroy evidence of the crime.

Regardless of whether this last report is true, those who knew of the old place certainly believed it to be haunted. The house has since been torn down, and no spirits have been reported in the building that replaced it.

Ghost Town

Dubbed Sheldrake by early French settlers in the 1800s, the lumbering community housed more than a thousand residents. Sheldrake thrived for nearly forty years, but the land seemed cursed. One fire after another destroyed the town, and at last, in the mid-1920s, the remaining population moved four miles south to a new village, called Paradise. They left behind a vacant town on the northeastern coast of the Upper Peninsula—one that truly seems to live up to the term "ghost town."

"That land is haunted," said Regan Petersen's uncle, as their boat skirted the Lake Superior shoreline on its way to Sault Ste. Marie. He gestured toward a cluster of old and abandoned shacks and buildings.

"Cool," said Regan's kid brother. "Can we go there?"

Uncle Bob shook his head. "Nope. It's private property, off limits."

"What makes you think it's haunted?" asked Regan.

Her uncle laughed. "People have been talking about that place for a hundred years. Just about every roof you can see—and more—has a ghost living in it."

"What do you mean by that?" said Regan.

"Well, first, there's the old Hopkins House. It's most famous for a couple who was staying there and saw a ghost walk right through their bedroom. Then there's the Palmer House. I believe that one has lights turning on and off at all hours of the day and night—even though it's completely empty."

"You're making this up," Regan protested.

"No, I'm not," replied her uncle. "And those are just for starters. There's also the Smith House, which is haunted by the ghost of an old logger. The Strobel house is visited by the spirit of a teacher. And the Biehl house is said to be known for the ghost of a beautiful woman."

"Hey, look," exclaimed Regan's brother. "There's somebody over there!"

The passengers glanced toward a dock that jutted into the Great Lake. An old sea captain stood, wearing a cape and smoking a pipe.

The three relatives waved to him, and the captain lifted his arm to wave back. But as he did so, his image slowly faded away. He vanished before the passengers' very eyes!

Uncle Bob turned toward his stunned niece. He smiled triumphantly. "See? I told you so."

Bewitched Blaze

It was known as the Battenfield House, and residents of Fife Lake—a popular tourist spot southeast of Grand Traverse Bay—knew its story well.

"The home once belonged to a notorious murderer," said an elderly townsman, eager to share his bizarre tale. "A disturbed woman who craved attention, she poisoned her family over the course of several years, reveling in the sympathy and affection that she received after each death. Many of her victims were relatives living in different places, but two of the deceased were immediate family, and their deaths occurred inside the Battenfield House—which now harbors a ghostly guest."

He hesitated, looking into the eyes of each of the seven tourists, ensuring that he had their undivided attention. Feeling certain that he did, the man continued.

"I've been inside the Battenfield House once—and only once," the old storyteller admitted. "I crept in there alone on a dare, and I saw the strangest sight I've ever laid my eyes upon."

He paused, and his audience collectively leaned forward in dreadful anticipation.

"I was sneaking upstairs when it happened. My friends were outside, and I was supposed to wave at them from a second-level window. It seemed easy enough, but I never thought . . ." The man stopped, acting as if the burden of sharing this strange story was too great.

"What?" exclaimed an attentive young man of about twenty, whose excitement got the better of him.

The elderly townsman chuckled softly. He took a deep breath and pressed onward. "Well, like I said, I was on my way upstairs. Suddenly, the newel post in front of me burst into flame! My gut told me to get out of there as fast as I could. But I figured—even though I hadn't started the fire—if the house burned down, I'd be in a heap of trouble."

"What did you do?" a second listener asked.

"The flame wasn't too big, so I thought I could manage it. I pulled off my shirt and tried to smother it. I expected to end up with a bit of a burn on my hands too. But that fire, it didn't have any heat. And when that blaze went out—by itself, mind you—it didn't leave any burn marks. None at all. Not on my hands and not on my shirt."

His audience stared at the old man. Their expressions suggested they weren't sure whether or not to believe him.

"How is that possible?" someone asked.

"I don't know. I didn't stick around to see. I ran out of that house as fast as my legs would carry me, and I never looked back."

Supernatural Sightings

Ghosts were the last thing on the Reinke family's mind when they moved into their new home in the small, central Michigan town of Harrison. They never could've guessed that they had taken residence in one of the state's most haunted houses.

Mrs. Reinke had just returned from the grocery store. She was filling the cupboards with food when she turned around—and gasped.

"What are you doing here?" she exclaimed, staring at the unfamiliar twin girls who stood before her. They must have been less than six years old.

Mrs. Reinke paused to ponder the strange scene, trying to imagine who the children were and how they came to be inside her home.

Suddenly, they started toward her, their hands clasped together as if playing a game of Red Rover.

Instinctively, Mrs. Reinke took a step back, but there was no room to maneuver. Before she fully realized what was happening, the girls were upon her.

An instant later, they were behind her. The children had passed right *through* her!

A terrible chill swept over Mrs. Reinke. Her entire body shuddered as she spun around. The twins disappeared through the wall and into the back yard. Mrs. Reinke raced to the window, but the children had vanished.

In another instance, her husband was behind their home, tying his boat to the dock on Budd Lake. Finishing his task, he stood and turned toward the house. A blur of motion caught his eye in the upstairs bedroom window.

"What in the world?" Mr. Reinke muttered.

Standing in the room, looking down at him, was the ghostly figure of a large, heavyset man.

Mr. Reinke raced into the house and up to his bedroom. He burst inside. But as he looked around, no one could be found. Fearing that he had imagined the entire episode, he decided not to tell a soul.

A few nights later, one of the Reinkes' children, their daughter, was awakened by a strange light coming from within her closet. The scared young girl shrieked. She buried her head under the covers.

Hoping the light was gone, she slowly lowered her blanket. What she saw next was far worse than a spooky light. The frightful specter of a large, heavyset man was standing at the foot of her bed.

"Mom! Dad!" she screamed, trembling and crying.

Her parents rushed to her bedroom, but by the time they arrived, the spirit was gone.

When Mr. Reinke heard the description of what his daughter had seen, he realized that it matched his own ghostly sighting. He later confided in his wife about his strange encounter.

The resident ghost, however, did not seem content just appearing to household members. The next day, when the Reinkes' daughter returned home from playing, she made a startling discovery.

"My room!" the girl screamed. "What happened to my room?"

She stood frozen in place, staring bewilderedly at her belongings. They had been emptied from her closet and scattered across the bedroom floor.

The Reinkes' son also had an encounter with the spirit. One evening, while playing in his bedroom, he heard a disturbing noise in the attic above. The sound could only be described as a bouncing rubber ball.

Its incessant *thump, thump, thump* annoyed the boy, and at last, he'd heard enough.

"Stop!" he hollered upward.

It worked. The sound came to an abrupt end.

Paranormal activity in the home slowed after that. The encounters were fewer and much less intense. The family eventually grew accustomed to their ghost. However, for friends and relatives, the Reinke house remained a frightful place to visit.

Bedeviled Businesses

Businesses

and Public Places

The Butler Did It

Few individuals are as synonymous with their home states as Henry Ford is with Michigan. In 1914, he changed the country (and the world) forever, when he began mass-producing his automobiles in assembly lines. Furthermore, he doubled his workers' wages, a move that garnered him national attention.

The resulting stream of reporters and job seekers knocking on his door led Ford and his family to retreat from their Detroit home. They purchased 1,300 acres of land in Dearborn and had a mansion built upon it—a house that would one day harbor a ghost.

In 1947, Ford died in his home. His estate changed hands several times, and a segment of it eventually became a museum. It is here, inside his mansion, where most of the paranormal activity has been reported.

Cheryl Martin is among the many who claim to have encountered a ghostly presence. While touring the mansion one summer afternoon, she noticed a sudden chill, one that caused her to shudder.

"Brrr," she said to a member of her group. "I wonder why it's so cold in here."

Cheryl shrugged it off, rubbing her arms to warm herself as she continued on the tour. The cold spells came and went, not just for her but for the entire group.

A short time later, the woman heard rushed footsteps echoing through a distant hallway. She couldn't help but wonder why someone here might be in such a hurry. She imagined all sorts of emergencies. (Of course, none came close to the actual reason for the sound.)

As the steps drew nearer, Cheryl and the others in her party turned to see a man hurrying toward them. He was dressed professionally, albeit old-fashioned, and he looked frantic, as if he were late for an important meeting.

Yet despite the man's quick pace, he never reached the tour group. Much to the spectators' surprise and horror, the stranger began to come apart. At first, his body seemed to blur. Then pieces of him began to disappear. Slowly, he dissolved into a cloud of mist, and in a matter of seconds, he had vanished completely.

Cheryl stared in bewildered astonishment at the spot where the man had been. Then slowly, she turned to read the expressions worn by the others in her party.

"Did I just see that?" someone asked, rhetorically.

Cheryl nodded, as did several others. No one seemed capable of speaking the word, "Yes."

Later in the day, while Cheryl studied old photos of the building, she made a discovery that shook her to the core. "That's him!" she yelled, pointing at a man in the picture. "That's the guy we saw."

Sure enough, it looked exactly like the ghost that had been in the hallway and had vanished. However, it wasn't Henry Ford. The apparition, as it turned out, was the Ford family's butler.

Reportedly, this specter is not alone. Rumors of other spirits roaming the premises have also surfaced, due in part to the historic items on display within the house and in the nearby Greenfield Village. The ghostly figures of the Fords, Abraham Lincoln and John F. Kennedy—to name a few—are said to have been seen there. (One witness even noted that President Kennedy told him, "There was more than one gunman.")

Some of these accounts may be questionable, but a vast number of witnesses claim to have encountered a supernatural presence. This has led many to conclude that the ghost of Henry Ford's butler does indeed roam the mansion's halls, loyally serving his former employer, even in death.

Mansfield Mine

When it came to the spooky tales surrounding the old ghost town of Mansfield, Barbara Hahn was skeptical. But she couldn't dispute the site's rich—albeit tragic—history.

The story of Mansfield began in 1889, when W.S. Calhoune discovered iron ore. Workers and their families flocked to the area for an opportunity to earn a living. Mansfield, located in the south-central part of the Upper Peninsula, grew to a population of nearly 400 residents in the years that followed.

By 1893, six side shafts had been dug into the Mansfield mine. Each was at a different depth, but all ran beneath the Michigamme River, a fact that would seal the fate of too many miners.

The tragic night arrived on September 28, 1893. While it is uncertain exactly how the events unfolded, most believe that the fifth level of the mine caved in. Since all of the shafts above it had been almost completely mined out, the first collapse caused a chain reaction. Level after level fell upon each other, until the waters of the river eventually deluged the workers below.

At the sixth level, the night boss heard the cave-ins above. "Get to the ladder, now!" he ordered his crew.

A downdraft caused all of the lanterns to extinguish, so the men felt their way through the pitch-black tunnels. Four miners never made it.

As for the rest, they climbed upward, through a flood of pouring river water, stopping at each level to breathe before entering the torrent again. It was a life-or-death struggle, but thanks to the night boss's leadership and his quick thinking, the men eventually surfaced, alive.

Unfortunately, the other crew working inside wasn't so lucky. Trapped within the flooded mines, a total of 27 men lost their lives on that fateful night.

Now, Barbara and her husband stood in what was left of the ghost town: a bridge and a handful of houses. The couple paid tribute to history at the granite monument, honoring the miners who died more than a century ago.

After a moment's pause, the Hahns moved onward, strolling amidst Mansfield's remains. From the distance, like an echo, Barbara heard the repeated clinks of a pick hitting rock. It was followed by a few faint screams.

She looked at her husband. "Do you hear that?"

"Hear what?" he replied.

"Never mind."

The sounds ceased, leaving Barbara to wonder if it had all been her imagination.

She didn't wonder long.

As she stepped closer to the river's dark waters, she noticed a small cluster of lights shining upward from below. She pointed and said, "Please, tell me you see that."

Her husband stared at the strange phenomenon, dumbfounded. Slowly, he nodded. "Yeah, I see it."

The couple quickened their pace, eager to investigate. As they drew closer, staring into the deep river water, the lights became clearer. Instead of a cluster of lights, the Hahns now saw many small but distinct orbs—27 of them.

"Looks like mining helmets," noted Barbara's husband.

Nothing else needed to be said. Understanding that they were witnessing something supernatural, the two of them stood silently for several minutes, watching until the last of the lights extinguished.

Calls in the Night

"It's not so bad," said Virginia Randall.

"It's old and worn," noted her husband, Warren. "You deserve better."

"It offers a bed and a roof. That's all we need, as long as we're together," Virginia added, optimistically. "Besides, it's only temporary."

And so, in 1907, the decision was made: The happy couple made their move from Detroit to Grand Rapids, taking residence in the run-down, mansion-sized boarding house that was known to locals as the Judd-White House. Warren worked a good job as a brakeman for the Grand Rapids & Indiana Railroad, so the couple's future looked bright, despite the relatively poor living conditions.

Tragically, less than a year later, the Randalls' dreams were quashed in one fateful moment: Warren lost his leg in an unfortunate accident. Even with an artificial wooden leg, the depressed man was unable to work—and his life slowly spiraled out of control.

Feeling discouraged and inept, Warren's mental state deteriorated. He grew paranoid and violent. He began to suspect that his wife was having an affair, and he snapped.

"I'll kill you," he yelled, wielding a straight razor.

Virginia screamed. Fearing for her life, she retreated out of the old boarding house and raced into the alley.

Despite his handicap, Warren had grown fairly nimble. He raced after her, and had he caught her, he likely would have murdered her. Luckily, Virginia escaped with her life. She decided not to press charges against him.

Sadly, however, this was not an isolated incident. In the coming months, the police were called to the Randalls' place countless times to break up fight after fight.

Virginia eventually decided that she had taken enough abuse. It broke her heart to do so, but she left her husband and moved out of the Judd-White House.

Warren was devastated. He told himself that he could not live without his beloved wife. He tirelessly pursued her, trying to win her back.

At first, Virginia resisted, choosing to have nothing to do with her estranged husband. But finally, in the summer of 1910, the woman agreed to an evening buggy ride with him. He was, after all, her "soul mate."

No one knows exactly what happened next, but the Randalls eventually ended up at the Judd-White House once more. Perhaps the evening was going well, and Virginia consented to the visit. Or maybe she was forced there against her will, under the threat of violence. Regardless, it seems apparent that the two of them had one final argument inside their home—an argument that ended when Warren removed his wooden leg and beat Virginia unconscious with it.

To finish her off—if he could not have her, no one would—Warren sealed the bedroom shut, using towels to block every opening. He ripped open a gas fixture, allowing his wife to be suffocated by the lethal fumes. And then he slashed his own throat with his straight razor.

For two weeks, the Randalls' bodies remained there, undiscovered. Then, finally, employees of a neighboring office building called the Board of Health, complaining of an awful, gaseous smell.

Investigators arrived at the Judd-White House and entered with a gas company employee. They were almost turned back by the terrible odor that greeted them: gas and rotting flesh. But the men pressed onward. Eventually they found their way to the bedroom, and at last, the gruesome scene was revealed.

Over the next decade, the house remained vacant—and for good reason. Many believed the restless spirits of Warren and Virginia Randall remained on the premises. Among other unexplained phenomena, several witnesses reported hearing the loud thump of Warren's wooden leg trudging across the floor. Others claimed to have heard the ghostly echo of Virginia's unanswered screams and calls for help.

Finally, in the early 1920s, the old boarding house was torn down. The Michigan Bell Telephone Company bought the land and built their offices upon it. Most believed it would mark an end to the hauntings.

It did not . . .

Brring!

"Not again," muttered Barney Hansen. He glanced at his clock, which told him it was 3:03 a.m.

Brring!

Barney rolled over in his bed and picked up the phone. "What do you want?"

It had become an almost nightly routine. Barney would be awakened by a ringing telephone. He would answer it, and no one on the other end would say a word.

Tonight was no different. Barney clicked the phone off and returned it to his nightstand.

He fell back into bed, considering what he had learned just a few days earlier: Barney was not the only one to be receiving these annoying prank phone calls. Several Grand Rapids residents were apparently on this joker's list—so many, in fact, that the police had gotten involved and were looking into the matter.

Brring!

Barney opened his eyes, surprised to now see sunlight shining into his room. He must have fallen asleep, although he didn't remember doing so.

He reached over and once again clutched the phone. "Hello?" he said, trying his best not to sound groggy.

He peeked at his clock: 9:37 a.m. *That's what I get for staying up past midnight,* Barney thought. *Oh, well, at least I have the day off.*

"Is this Barney Hansen?" said an authoritative voice through the telephone.

"Yes, speaking," Barney replied.

"Mr. Hansen, my name is Richard Sanders. I've been asked to contact you regarding your complaints about some late-night prank calls."

Barney sat up in bed, willing himself into alertness. "Yes, what about them?"

"Sir, we traced those phone calls during each of the past three nights. It seems that they're originating within the offices of the Michigan Bell Telephone Company."

"What?" Barney exclaimed. "So, why is the telephone

company calling me at all hours of the night?"

"That's the bizarre part, Mr. Hansen. No one is making those calls."

Barney paused for a moment, trying to process this latest statement. Unable to do so, he said, "I don't get what you mean."

"Sir, trust me when I tell you: We've spent nearly three days checking and double-checking our data. The calls did, in fact, come from within those offices. However—as impossible as this might sound—not a single person was inside the building or anywhere on the premises at the times the calls were placed."

Barney sat speechless, his mouth hanging open.

After a brief pause, the voice on the line broke the silence. "We believe these disturbances will cease within a week or two. If they do not, please contact us again."

With that, the conversation ended.

Left with no options, Barney waited, and in a matter of days, his patience was rewarded. The ghostly phone calls ended, and he was once again able to enjoy peaceful sleep. The mystery behind the strange phenomena, however, was never solved.

Genevive's Ghost

"I want it," Genevive Stickney demanded. "And I'm going to have it!" The heavyset woman had fallen in love with a glorious property on Old Mission Peninsula, the eighteen-mile strip of paradise that jutted north of Traverse City and into Grand Traverse Bay.

Genevive's husband, J.W. Stickney, wanted nothing more than to keep his jealous and temperamental wife happy, so he dipped into the fortune he'd made as a lumber baron and purchased the estate. The site was remodeled, and by the 1920s, the Chicago tycoons were using the place as their summer home.

Genevive spared no expense in lavishly decorating her dream house. She even had an elevator installed—a rare luxury! However, her most precious possession was a custom-made, gilt-edged mirror. The large woman spent countless hours staring at herself in the glass because it had been specifically designed to make whatever it reflected appear thinner.

As time passed, Genevive's health worsened. Her husband hired a nurse to care for his ailing wife, but Genevive was consumed by jealousy, fearing that J.W. would fall in love with the pretty young aide. Unfortunately for Genevive, her fears were realized. J.W. and the nurse began an illicit love affair.

To make matters worse, in a surprise twist of fate, J.W. died before his wife did. He left all of his riches to the nurse. Genevive was granted only her beloved house. The widow was so distraught that she reportedly committed suicide, hanging herself in the rafters above the elevator shaft. Thus, her restless spirit was released . . .

Mary Bobendrier stood in the second-floor hallway, admiring her reflection in a nearby mirror. The forty-two-year-old woman had been dining inside the Stickneys' old house, which was renovated in 1959 and turned into a restaurant known as Bowers Harbor Inn.

After eating a hearty meal, she was surprised to see such a slim reflection. "I've never looked better," the woman sang with a laugh. "I must've lost weight."

She continued to stare at herself in the gilt-edged mirror until a second woman peeked in behind her. Mary blushed at her own vanity.

"I'm sorry," Mary said with a shy grin. She spun on her heels to face the rotund woman. "It's just that I—" Mary choked off her words. The hallway behind her was empty.

She rushed downstairs in a panic, screaming that she had just seen the ghost of Genevive Stickney!

Along with Mary's sighting, countless other para-normal phenomena have been credited to Genevive's spirit. From flickering lights and moving objects to rapping sounds and locked doors opening without cause, the ghost that haunts Bowers Harbor Inn has made herself known. Even the old elevator, which hasn't run for years, has been reported to occasionally start by itself and move from floor to floor.

Bowers Harbor Inn remains one of Michigan's most haunted locales. In fact, it has gained national recognition and was reportedly even featured on an episode of the old television series *Unsolved Mysteries*.

Haunted Island

It's only natural that a tourist destination as popular and historic as Mackinac Island offers more than its share of legends and folklore. From a haunted military fort to Native American apparitions, Mackinac Island is home to dozens of ghostly tales. Not surprisingly, residents and visitors delight in hearing and retelling these accounts. Some even refer to Mackinac Island as "the most haunted area in Michigan." (Those with interests in the paranormal can take guided ghost tours.) Perhaps the most notorious spooky story of this Lake Huron locale stems from Pine Cottage, an elegant bed & breakfast built on Bogan Lane in the late 1800s.

According to most accounts, the ghost of Pine Cottage was born on a stormy night in 1942, when a woman was brutally slain on the premises.

Twenty years later, an eager entrepreneur purchased the property. He soon learned of the cottage's unexpected tenant, for spring brought with it more than just green grass and warmer temperatures.

To the owner's surprise, doors within Pine Cottage began opening and closing on their own. Unexplained footsteps were heard by staff members and visitors alike—in all corners of the cottage. Personal belongings began turning up in peculiar places (or disappearing altogether).

Later that year, the owner had a terrifying experience. He casually stepped into a room on the first floor, mindlessly going about his day's business.

Suddenly, the closet door flung open. The man glimpsed a blur of motion. He instinctively flinched before turning his full attention toward the movement. His eyes focused on a frantic, angry woman—except she couldn't possibly be a woman; she was only visible from the waist up!

She charged forward, not giving her victim time to react. The "woman" ran directly into him with the force of a linebacker, knocking the entrepreneur to the ground. He spun in time to see his assailant disappear out the window.

"What was that?" he muttered, barely believing the encounter had just occurred.

In the years that followed, the bed & breakfast's paranormal events continued. Several different-looking spirits were seen—the most common reports involving a male specter standing beside beds and a little girl roaming the house. Some witnesses also claimed to have spied a girl crying in the attic window.

Despite these strange happenings, the owner tolerated his haunted guests for more than 30 years. It wasn't until 1995 that he finally moved to another part of the state. As for Pine Cottage, it is still a popular destination for visitors to the island.

Trouble at the Theatre

Percy Francis loved his visits to Calumet—a quaint village in the northwest corner of the Upper Peninsula. Of course, Calumet was best known for its history as a mining town, but it was also the site of a notorious mass murder. Percy couldn't help but remember the gruesome details as he drove past the Italian Hall Historical Marker.

The fifty-six-year-old recalled what he knew about the 1913 Massacre. On Christmas Eve of that year, tensions were high between striking laborers and the mining companies. In hopes of raising the spirits of its members, the miners' labor union planned a holiday party on the second floor of the Italian Hall. Unfortunately, the event turned out to be anything but festive.

At around 4:30 p.m., with nearly 500 people (including women and children) inside the hall, an unidentified man yelled, "Fire!"

In a matter of moments, panic swept through the crowd. Miners and their families madly dashed toward the main exit: a narrow stairwell. Chaos ensued, and seventy-four people—including fifty-nine children—were crushed to death on the steps leading to the first floor.

There was no fire.

"Those poor children," Percy muttered, before shaking the memory from his head. He was here for much happier reasons. He was on his way to see a performance at the Calumet Theatre.

The renovated auditorium provided the perfect setting for such cultural events as symphonies, operas and more. Percy was especially thrilled whenever a folk festival came to town. He never missed one of them.

Admittedly, the middle-aged man was also aware of the site's "haunted" reputation. Most famously, in 1958, a young actress forgot her lines during a performance in front of a sold-out crowd. She gazed skyward, desperately trying to remember her part. Reportedly, the apparition of a deceased actress, Madame Helena Modjeska, appeared above her. Hidden from the crowd, the helpful specter fed the woman her lines, and the show was saved.

Modjeska, who had performed at the Calumet Theatre while still living, was believed to be the building's most active spirit. Her apparition had been seen a number of times. However, as Percy was about to find out, Madame Modjeska was not alone . . .

He was inside the Calumet Theatre, on his way toward the restroom when he first heard the scream.

Eeeee!

Percy would later joke that the cry almost stopped his heart, for it sounded as if someone were being tortured or murdered. He believed that he was unequipped to handle an emergency—whatever it might be—so Percy glanced up and down the hallway. Much to his dismay, he found that he was completely alone.

For a moment, Percy wrestled with himself, trying to decide if he were the type to blindly rush to a stranger's aid or if it might be wiser to wander the hallways, searching for an usher, a janitor, anyone.

Eeeee!

There isn't time, he decided.

Mustering all of the bravery he could, Percy raced toward the sound. He was so intent on locating its source that he momentarily forgot how scared he was.

Percy heard the scream again, closer now. "I'm coming," he shouted. He immediately regretted it. *If a girl is being attacked,* he thought, *I just warned her attacker to expect me.*

Nevertheless, Percy charged onward as fast as his legs would take him. He reached the source of the screams in less than a minute. But as he raced to the victim's aid, he did not find what he expected.

It wasn't a woman, hurt or beaten. It wasn't a medical emergency. It wasn't even a lost child—at least, not in the sense Percy would have imagined.

The wannabe hero stopped in his tracks. His mouth went dry, and his knees buckled. His eyes grew wide as he stared into the face of a ghost: the apparition of an innocent young girl.

She smiled sweetly and waved at Percy. He tried to wave back, but his arm muscles would not obey him. Instead, he simply gawked at the spirit, watching as her transparent figure slowly faded to nothing.

A few minutes later, as he trudged away from the scene, Percy once more remembered the tragedy at the Italian Hall. He silently wondered if he had just met a victim of the 1913 Massacre.

School Spirit

Beatrice Feckers was new to Ann Arbor's Huron High School. With aspirations to be a movie star, it made sense for her to transfer to one of the top high schools in Michigan (and in the entire country, for that matter). By all accounts, Beatrice's thick dark hair and big brown eyes gave her the "look" of a Hollywood starlet. As a member of the Huron Players club, she would have an opportunity to participate in every aspect of theater production, from acting and special effects to publicity and fundraising.

She stepped into the school theater, eager to meet her fellow thespians, but the auditorium was almost empty. The only other person was a young woman, wearing a light pink dress, walking along the catwalk above the stage.

Beatrice marched forward enthusiastically. "Hello," she called.

The girl in pink ignored her.

Beatrice continued closer. Assuming that she had not been heard, she spoke more loudly. "Excuse me."

Still, the stranger on the catwalk did not respond.

Beatrice waited until she was at the edge of the stage before calling upward again. This time she almost shouted.

"Hi, my name is Beatrice Feckers. I'm new here."

"Who are you talking to?" came the reply. But it wasn't from the girl above. The voice was male, and its source was behind her.

Beatrice spun to see a handsome young man, tall and muscular, walking down the aisle toward her. His blue eyes sparkled, and he was all smiles as he awaited her reply.

Beatrice felt her cheeks flush. "Oh, hi," she muttered, trying to regain her composure. "I was actually talking to her." She gestured toward the catwalk, but the girl in pink could no longer be seen. "That's odd," Beatrice noted. "She was up there a second ago."

"Who?" asked the teenaged boy.

"A girl, she was standing right there." Beatrice pointed upward again.

The boy's eyes widened. He looked more astonished than Beatrice thought he should.

"No way," he exclaimed. "Was she wearing a pink dress?"

Beatrice nodded. "Yes, I think so. Why?"

"You're so lucky. You just saw Mary."

The new student offered the stranger a sideways glance. "And why does that make me lucky?"

The boy laughed. "Oh, sorry. I suppose I should clue you in."

"That would be nice," Beatrice replied.

"As I understand it, Mary was a student here in the late 1970s. She was big into theater and liked to help out however she could. One day, after school, she was up on that catwalk working on some light fixtures for a show. No one knows exactly how it happened, but she somehow slipped and fell. She landed headfirst on the stage and died."

"So the girl I saw is—" Beatrice began to say.

"A ghost," the boy finished. "Only a handful of people have ever seen her. I guess now you're one of them."

The young man, who finally introduced himself as Tony, boldly grabbed Beatrice's hand and led her backstage. "Come on," he said. "There's something I want to show you."

They entered the towering prop room together, and Beatrice immediately noticed name after name spray painted on the wall. She looked at Tony, bemused.

"It's a school tradition," said the boy. "The seniors add their names after their last play."

Beatrice shrugged. "All right, but why are you showing me this?"

"Mary died before her last show, so her name shouldn't be here."

"If you say so," answered Beatrice.

Tony nodded. "I do. But take a look at that."

The wall must have been about twenty-five feet tall. Tony pointed to a spot high upon it.

Beatrice followed his finger with her eyes, turning her gaze upward. She gasped.

Painted in bold red letters, upside down, about six feet from the top, was the name "Mary." It was as if the person who painted it had been standing with her feet planted firmly on the ceiling.

Eerie Outdoors

Lost in the Woods

"Hello?" Roland Jackson shouted. "Can anybody hear me? I need help!"

No one answered.

The hunter cursed himself silently as he glanced left, then right. How had he gotten himself into this mess? How had he lost the rest of his group?

By his own admission, Roland didn't know the forest area outside Oscoda very well, and yet he had foolishly wandered off alone. Now, as the sun set against the distant horizon, he saw only the silhouettes of unfamiliar trees in every direction.

His heart began to race. His mind conjured images of bears and coyotes lurking in the shadows, waiting to attack. Roland gripped his shotgun more tightly, but it did little to calm his nerves. The thick forest that enveloped Roland seemed to draw closer, squeezing him. He felt as if he were being buried alive.

"I have to get out of here," the man said to himself. Then he shouted, "Help! Somebody help me!"

Roland darted through the forest, desperate to find an escape, but his luck failed him. Several long hours later, with the moon almost directly overhead, the exhausted hunter collapsed to the forest floor. He resigned himself to spending the night there, and he tried to make himself as comfortable as possible.

Suddenly—to Roland's surprise—a beautiful young woman appeared from behind a nearby tree. She was tall and fit, like a runner. Her hair was long and brown, her eyes a deep green.

The woman gasped in apparent surprise upon spying the stranger, but she composed herself quickly. "What are you doing here?" she asked, a subtle giggle suggesting that she already knew.

Roland answered anyway. "I'm lost." He was tired and felt chilled to the core, but the woman's smile was a warm summer breeze.

"My name is Leona," she said. "My family owns a farm not far from here, so I know these woods pretty well. I'd be happy to show you to the road, if you'd like."

The hunter jumped to his feet, his energy restored—if only for a moment. "I'd be grateful. I thought I'd have to sleep out here tonight."

Leona led Roland away, and within an hour, they passed through a final stand of trees and out of the forest. The hunter was overwhelmed with relief to see a familiar road less than twenty feet away.

"Do you think you can you find your way from here?" Leona asked.

"The cabin we're staying in is right down the road, so I'll be fine. Thank you so much for your help." He reached out to shake Leona's hand.

She smiled at the hunter.

And then she vanished before his eyes.

Later, when Roland recounted the story to his hunting buddies, they didn't believe him. And when he called his wife to tell her, she didn't know what to say. However, at a local bar the next night, Roland told his strange tale again.

The bartender rolled his head back and laughed. "It's not the first time I've heard that one," the bartender said. "Leona is well known around these parts."

Roland eyed the bartender suspiciously. "What do you mean by that?"

"It's true enough that Leona lived with her family on a farm near those woods. And it's true that she still wanders the forest, helping people who need it. But that wasn't Leona you saw. She died back in 1929 after a hunter mistook her for a deer. You met Leona's ghost."

The Ada Witch

Sara crept through the thick, dark woods outside the western Michigan town of Ada. She whispered her lover's name. "Dean? Dean, are you here?"

"Sara," came a gentle voice from out of the darkness. "Of course I am. Have I ever stood you up?"

Dean stepped forward, and the two lovers embraced, kissing each other in a frenzied moment of passion.

An instant later, their desire was interrupted.

"Sara! How dare you?" a familiar voice shouted from behind the woman.

Having long suspected his wife of cheating, Sara's husband had feigned sleep that night. When she'd finally snuck away from their bed, he followed her here.

Now, consumed with jealousy, he rushed toward Sara and violently bashed her head with a small log, killing her.

Next, the vengeful man turned his attention toward Dean, but the two men were evenly matched. Both suffered serious injuries, which eventually led to their deaths.

It was a tragic ending for the trio. However, Sara's tale was not yet finished . . .

Jaron and Angela crept along the dirt road, up the hill toward Findlay Cemetery. The surrounding trees made the two explorers feel completely isolated.

"Man, this place is freaky," said Angela.

"That's the idea," Jaron noted with a smirk.

It was well past midnight, but the duo's flashlights, as well as the full moon, offered enough illumination for the college-aged students to navigate their way into the grave-yard. They were here for one reason: to see the Ada Witch.

"Why is she called a witch, anyway?" Angela asked. "She's just a ghost, right?"

Jaron nodded. "Ada Witch has a better ring to it."

"So it's a sexist thing," Angela protested, half joking. "She's a woman, so that makes her a witch."

"Oh, good, here comes another rant," replied Jaron, shaking his head with a chuckle.

A second later, their playfulness ceased.

"Sara! How dare you?" an angry voice shouted in the distance.

The startling noise was immediately followed by a bloodcurdling scream—one that ended abruptly.

"Did you hear that?" said a wide-eyed Angela.

"Uh-huh," answered Jaron. "Let's see if we can get a closer look."

He stealthily inched toward the mysterious sounds. Three steps. Five steps. Twelve steps. Jaron stopped. He tilted his head slightly, listening for another noise.

He felt a tap on his shoulder, and he spun quickly to see what Angela wanted. "What?" he asked.

She wasn't there.

She still stood twelve paces back, having remained motionless since they heard the violent, ghostly exchange.

"Okay, that's a little weird," Jaron said to himself. Then he addressed Angela. "Are you coming?"

Reluctantly, she started toward her companion. But as Jaron watched, waiting for her to join him, he saw a look of pure terror wash over her face. Angela stopped moving forward and instead began to back away from him. The blood seemed to drain from her face, and she muttered something Jaron couldn't comprehend.

He followed her gaze over his shoulder, and when he turned to look behind him, Jaron was shocked to see a misty blue figure floating in his direction.

His muscles tensed, and his mouth dropped open. "Oh, wow," he whispered.

The glowing blue object stopped about ten yards away, and for the briefest of moments, Jaron caught a glimpse of a beautiful, dark-haired woman within the blue shape. She was wearing a long white gown. Then, just as quickly, the beautiful specter morphed into the ghastly form of a woman who had been beaten to death.

The sight caused Jaron to turn away for a moment. When he looked again, the mysterious blue object was gone.

"Did you see that?" Jaron asked Angela, excitedly. He glanced back toward her; she was shielding her eyes.

"No!" she demanded. "Is it gone?"

Jaron hurried over to his terrified friend and wrapped his arm around her. "Yeah, she's gone. Let's go home."

He led Angela out of the haunted graveyard, eager to share this bizarre encounter with his friends.

Hell's Bridge

"What are we doing here?" Bonnie Simms asked her blue-eyed boyfriend.

"It's Halloween night," Nathan replied. "I wanted to try something different."

Bonnie couldn't argue with that. This was certainly a departure from their normal routine of renting a movie and ordering a pizza. They had driven past Algoma Township and onto a long, desolate dirt road, which ran beside the Rogue River. As if that weren't enough, they had parked their car in the middle of nowhere and had hiked into the woods. Their trail led them to an old iron bridge, on which they now stood.

The setting alone was enough to give Bonnie the creeps: The darkness and isolation, trees enveloping them in every direction, it was almost too much to take. Bonnie couldn't help but conjure up memories of her favorite horror flick, *The Blair Witch Project*, which only added to her terror.

She checked her watch; it was nearing midnight. "So, what's the story of this place, again?" she asked. She didn't really want to be reminded, but anything was better than the sound of silence.

Nathan checked his own watch. "It's almost time. Are you ready to be scared?"

Bonnie laughed sarcastically. "Are you kidding? Look around. I'm already scared."

Nathan smiled triumphantly. "The story goes that a man named Elias Friske used to live around these parts, way back in the 1800s. He went crazy and murdered a bunch of kids. Their bodies were supposedly found right here, on this stretch of river."

"Is it true?" Bonnie asked, nervously.

"Yeah, I think so. And get this: Later, when they caught the guy, he said a demon made him do it."

Bonnie swallowed hard. "Good story. Can we go now?"

"Just wait. I'm not finished," said Nathan. "Rumor has it that, in the early hours of morning, fishermen on the river have seen a ghostly figure standing right here. And at the stroke of midnight, if you're on this bridge, you can hear the devil laughing."

"All right, stop. I've heard enough," Bonnie whispered. "Let's go home."

Nathan checked his watch again. "It's just a few more minutes. And don't worry; I sincerely doubt we're going to hear anything."

Against her better judgment, Bonnie waited for three minutes until her watch struck midnight. When nothing happened, she waited with Nathan for six more.

"See?" he finally said. "I told you there was nothing to worry about."

Bonnie breathed a deep sigh of relief. It was just a story, and there was no reason to be afraid. She could enjoy the nice Halloween scare that Nathan had provided— a great memory and a funny story to share with her friends.

Suddenly, the night's stillness was interrupted—not by the devil's cackle but by a sound just as terrifying.

Children crying.

Bonnie gasped. "Do you hear that?"

Nathan didn't reply. He simply stared at her, his pale face and shocked expression revealing his own fright.

Bonnie grabbed his hand. "Nathan, come on."

He nodded, as if slowly awakening from a trance. Then he hurried his girlfriend off Hell's Bridge and away from that horrifying noise—a chilling end to a night Nathan and Bonnie would never forget.

Mill Pond Menace

Mill Pond Park was haunted. At least, that's what everyone said. Kristy Hartman wasn't about to disagree. After dark, that place totally gave her the creeps. Still, her boyfriend, Rick, wanted to check it out. He claimed that he was into ghost hunting, but Kristy figured it was just a macho guy thing.

A story had been circulating around Mount Pleasant about a group of college students who visited Mill Pond in 2006. While exploring the park one night, a nineteen-year-old girl had a bizarre vision: a waking dream about a demonic force trying to scratch her and her friends.

Later that night, one of her companions called with a chilling discovery. Upon returning to his place, he found claw marks on the side of his body.

Now, as Kristy strolled through the park with Rick, she wondered if they might experience their own ghostly event.

"You're right," Rick admitted. "This place is freaky."

"I know," whispered Kristy. "It feels like somebody's watching us—like we're not alone." She felt a shudder run through her body, and she nuzzled closer to her boyfriend.

"Any scary visions yet?" he said, half joking.

Kristy shook her head. She didn't even want to think about it. They had already crossed the Chippewa River and were hiking deeper into the wooded park. The ninety acres that surrounded them were a stark reminder of how far away help would be—if they needed it.

"Look," said Rick. "Someone's coming." He gestured toward a person walking in their direction.

Kristy noted the relief in his voice. Maybe Rick wasn't so macho, after all.

The hiker drew closer, and Rick shouted, "Hello."

No reply came. The stranger simply marched onward.

Suddenly, Kristy's instincts screamed, "Stop!" She obeyed them.

Rick halted beside her. "What is it?" he asked, although a slight quiver revealed his alarm, as well.

"He's just a black shape," Kristy quietly replied. "We should be able to make out his features by now. Right?"

"It's dark," said Rick.

"Not that dark. I can't even see his eyes."

As if in response to that final statement, the stranger's eyes glowed to life—two deep red orbs!

Kristy couldn't help herself. She screamed. Then she turned and ran. Rick ran too—so fast and so hard that he disappeared ahead of his girlfriend, leaving her far behind.

Afraid to look back, Kristy continued her surge forward. She feared that she would feel a cold, bony grip on her neck at any instant. But it never came.

When she reached the parking lot, she finally stopped running. Waiting by his car, Rick smiled weakly and invited her into the passenger seat.

Kristy ignored him. She walked home.

The Michigan Dogman

It was supposed to be an April Fool's Day joke. Jack O'Malley, host of WTCM radio's morning show in Traverse City, wanted to prank his listeners. So program director Steve Cook recorded a song about a half-man, half-dog creature that roamed northern Michigan, terrorizing the communities. Both O'Malley and Cook believed the melodic number to be a work of fiction. They were wrong.

On April 1, 1987, Cook's song "The Legend" premiered on WTCM. The phone calls soon followed.

"That song you played, it scared me," said the first caller. His voice carried the crisp, raspy tone of a long-lived life. "It reminded me of something I saw years ago."

The elderly man was one of many Michiganders to share their bizarre Dogman encounters, and "The Legend" became a favorite tune of WTCM listeners.

Three months later, the Dogman struck outside the town of Luther. This time, it left evidence. A forest ranger and a police officer were called to a log cabin in the woods. They were flabbergasted by what they found.

"Look at those marks around the doors and windows," said one of the men. "He tried to chew his way in."

"Yeah, and his claws must be razor sharp," noted the other. "The scratches are more than an inch deep."

"What kind of animal did this? A bear?"

"I've never seen a bear leave tracks like that!"

Shockingly, the only animal prints the men could find looked like those of a very large dog.

After that, the legend of the Michigan Dogman picked up steam, eventually being carried nationally. However, as with most sensational stories, interest soon faded. Until . . .

A new creature emerged in southeastern Wisconsin— one that was eerily similar to Michigan's monster.

Reports began with a farmer who spotted an over-sized "dog" stalking his cattle. Soon, there were dozens of eyewitness accounts outside the town of Elkhorn, less than 200 miles from Luther, as the crow flies. This version of the Dogman came to be known as the Bray Road Beast (since most of its known activity occurred on or near Bray Road).

September of 1989 marked the first sighting, but the most frightening encounter happened on Halloween night, 1991. Doris Gipson drove along Bray Road, distracted by her car's radio. The teenaged girl leaned forward to change the station.

Thump!

Her right front tire surged up then down. Doris gripped the steering wheel and slammed on the brakes.

"Oh, no," she whispered, glancing behind her to see what she had hit. The road was empty.

Fearing that she had injured someone's pet dog—or worse—she climbed out of her vehicle and peered into the cold darkness.

"Hello?" she called, if for no other reason than to break the eerie silence.

Suddenly, as if from nowhere, a muscular, hairy form leapt onto the road and dashed straight toward her. Doris retreated to her vehicle. She jumped inside, slammed the door closed behind her and quickly locked the doors.

Clang!

The creature greedily clutched the trunk of Doris's car.

The teenaged girl screamed and, pressing her foot against the gas pedal, shifted the car into drive.

Behind her, she heard the sharp whistle of claws scratching against metal, as the beast—unable to maintain its grip—fell backward.

Later that evening, Doris returned to the scene, this time driving with a girl she had taken trick-or-treating.

"You would not believe what happened to me a few hours ago," said Doris. "I hit a bear, and it tried to maul me."

"No way," replied her young passenger. "Really?"

"Wait," whispered Doris, suddenly afraid to speak at full volume. "The bear's still here." She gestured up ahead, toward a large form on the side of the road.

"Let's get out of here, Doris."

"No argument from me," she said.

As Doris accelerated away from the beast for the second time that night, her passenger peeked outside the window. When they were safely away, she turned to Doris and said, "I don't think that was a bear."

In the years that followed these paranormal events, reported sightings of the Michigan Dogman and the Bray Road Beast slowed, but they never stopped. To this day, a handful of encounters are reported every year in the areas surrounding Luther and Elkhorn. It seems apparent that something is out there. Whether or not the two monsters are one and the same remains a mystery.

Traveler
Terrors

Car Trouble

It was a chilly November night in 2007, when Don Winter dropped off his daughter at Farmers Alley Theatre in Kalamazoo. He walked the teenaged girl inside for play rehearsal, then returned to his minivan, unlocked the doors and hopped into the driver's seat.

As he did so, he noticed the overpowering smell of fast food coming from within. The scent was out of place, since Don and his daughter had eaten at home, but the forty-year-old man didn't dwell on it. In fact, it probably would have escaped his memory all together, except for what happened when he started his vehicle: the wipers, the air conditioner and the radio blasted him.

The explosion of noise and motion jolted Don, but his nerves settled soon enough. Ignoring his certainty that the minivan's doors had been locked, he imagined a trickster teen, toting a bagful of burgers, giggling at the prank he had pulled.

Don put his vehicle into reverse, backed out of his parking spot and drove forward into the evening's darkness. He left the city lights behind him as he headed north on Douglas Avenue toward his rural home, not far from

Cooper Cemetery. Memories of the earlier scare dominated his thoughts, but this evening's frights were over.

At least, that's what Don believed.

The driver glanced into his rearview mirror, and he received his second jolt of the evening. Something moved behind him, something *inside* his minivan.

Immediately, he recalled the old campfire story that ended with a homicidal maniac hiding in the backseat of the car. Don quickly turned on his interior lights and looked backward. No one was there.

It must be my imagination, Don thought. He convinced himself that he hadn't seen anything and that he was, in fact, alone.

He didn't stay convinced for long.

Just four miles from home, the minivan's "door ajar" light shone to life. The vehicle's sensors indicated that the rear, hatchback door had been opened.

Don's heart began to race. Someone else was inside the minivan, hiding behind the backseat. The driver once again turned on the interior lights. This time he shouted, "Hello? I know you're in here!"

There was no reply.

Instead, Don heard a loud *thump!*

It was followed by another.

He weighed his options. He could pull over, or he could continue home. If someone else were in the vehicle, stopping would leave the two of them alone in the dark. But if he kept going, he could at least pull into his garage and arm himself with a baseball bat.

Neither option sounded particularly good, but Don found himself favoring the second, if only because it meant he didn't have to do anything—yet.

Don chose to delay the fearful encounter, continuing on his way. In fact he accelerated, half hoping that a police officer would pull him over for speeding.

Within minutes, Don reached his gravel driveway and, turning onto it, kept a close watch on his rearview mirror. After all, this would most likely be the time when his stow-away would act: either to attack him or to jump out the back and run for it.

The driver inched his minivan closer to home, pushing the ceiling console button that activated the garage door. He maintained a watchful eye on the backseat of his vehicle, and still there was no movement.

The confrontation was drawing nearer. Don became certain that his heart would beat right out of his chest. As his minivan entered the garage, Don stole a quick glance at the barrel in the far left corner, where his family's foot-balls, basketballs and—most importantly—a wooden bat were stored.

Short of breath and shaking with fright, Don decided the time was now. He carefully unlatched his seatbelt and threw the minivan into park. In one fluid motion, he flung open the door and leapt onto the concrete. Don dashed to the barrel and withdrew his bat. He wheeled toward the vehicle, and he waited.

Minutes passed. Nothing happened. Surprisingly, Don felt his fear turn to impatience. Perhaps it was adrenaline, or perhaps it was the false sense of security that the bat provided, but Don decided to take a closer look.

He clutched the bat with both hands, lifted it over his head and crept toward the rear of his vehicle. As he passed the back tire, he leaned forward and peeked around the corner. The hatchback door was fully closed.

Don peered through the window beside him, but try as he might, he couldn't see anyone inside.

He took a deep breath, calmed his shivering hands and stepped behind the minivan. He grabbed the door, pulled it open and jumped backward, putting a safe distance between himself and . . .

. . . an empty trunk?

No one else was there.

Don quickly scanned the area, and he even checked beneath the minivan. But he found no trace of anyone. Impossibly, his mysterious rider had vanished.

The revelation left Don shaken—perhaps even more so than if he had come face to face with an actual person. He tried to think of a reasonable explanation for the evening's events. He couldn't. Don had to admit that either the rider had hopped out at fifty-five miles per hour or he had just experienced an encounter with the supernatural.

The Woman in the Road

Henry Ruff Road had a reputation. It was considered unlucky. Running north and south outside the city of Westland in southeastern Michigan, Henry Ruff Road provided the setting for far too many car accidents— especially at the spot near William Ganong Cemetery (otherwise called Butler Cemetery).

That particular stretch of land struck Nathan Johnstone as creepy. Driving along the cursed road, he couldn't help but notice the area's desolate, neglected condition. Waist-high weeds, fallen trees and a rusty gate added to the graveyard's frightening aura. The fact that Nathan felt as if he were traveling through the most isolated place in the world didn't help matters, either.

It's weird, thought Nathan. *This is such a remote spot. How can it be the site of so many fender benders? Is this road really cursed?*

As if in response to his question, Nathan saw a woman dressed in white standing in the road directly ahead. He slammed on his breaks and braced for impact, nearly swerving into the ditch.

Nathan closed his eyes and ducked, waiting for the

thud of his car hitting the woman. But the sound never came. In fact, when Nathan opened his eyes, no one was there. The woman in white had vanished.

More than a little shaken, the driver sat in silence for a moment, trying to calm his nerves. Then he stepped out of his car to erase any doubt that he may have hit someone.

Nathan walked around his vehicle, noticing with dread that he had stopped directly in front of the frightful old cemetery. Fortunately, and much to his relief, he found no trace of anyone else near—or under—his car.

A chance glimpse toward the graveyard almost brought Nathan to his knees. His hands began to shake, and he gasped to catch his breath. Deep within William Ganong Cemetery, standing beside a monument, was the ghostly figure of a woman dressed in white.

Nathan fumbled his keys out of his pocket. As quickly as he could, he hopped back into his car, and he drove.

The Denton Demon

"It doesn't matter which story you believe," said Rob Bixby. "They both agree on one thing: Denton Road Bridge is haunted by the Denton Demon."

The teenager drove his parents' station wagon east, out of Ypsilanti, toward the haunted destination. Four of his closest friends rode with him.

"Personally," said D.J. Rhodes from the shotgun seat, "I like the one about the mom and her kid. A farmer came home one night and caught his wife in bed with another man from town."

"You would like this story," joked one of his friends from the backseat.

D.J. continued. "The farmer freaked out and murdered the man with a hammer. Next, he turned to kill his wife; she was already off and running. She grabbed their child, and they hid under the Denton Road Bridge."

"I think I know where this is going," chimed a second voice from behind.

"Right," D.J. replied. "The loony-tunes farmer found them. He viciously murdered them, right on the spot, and then he disappeared—never to be seen again."

"According to that story," added Rob, "he either killed himself or went into hiding. But the ghosts of his victims remain, appearing as balls of light that chase cars away from the bridge."

Within minutes, the daring teens turned north onto Denton Road. Not long thereafter, they reached the haunted locale. Rob parked the car atop the bridge, turned off the ignition and waited.

"So, what about the other story?" asked the third back-seat passenger. "How does that one go?"

"It's not nearly as interesting," admitted Rob. "But it's more likely to be true."

"It was a game of chicken," D.J. revealed, interrupting his friend. "Two kids were gunning for each other down this stretch of road."

"Yeah, but the loser lost more than his pride," noted Rob. "He died when his car crashed off the bridge."

It was D.J.'s turn again. "The weird thing is this version agrees about the balls of light chasing cars. But with this story, the balls of light are two phantom headlights."

Following this second account, the teenagers silently waited in their car atop the bridge. They remained there for several minutes. Nothing happened.

Finally, one of the boys said, "How long are we gonna sit here?"

"Right," said another. "I'm sure we'd look like idiots, if anyone could see us."

The consensus within the car quickly became, "This is boring." Rob started the vehicle, and the station wagon was soon on its way.

As the teens drove along Denton Road, toward Geddes Road, Rob made a startling discovery. He glanced into the rearview mirror and saw two bright headlights appear on the bridge, seemingly out of nowhere.

"Guys, check it out," he said. "There's a car back there."

"Probably the ghost," D.J. joked, as he and the others turned around to see.

Rob kept a close watch on the headlights, keeping one eye on the road and the other on his windshield's mirror. Much to his surprise and alarm, the headlights accelerated toward his station wagon.

"How fast are you going?" asked D.J., never taking his eyes off the lights behind them. "They're gaining on us." His voice revealed a hint of fear.

Rob glanced at the speedometer as he pressed his foot to the floor. Forty miles per hour. Fifty. Fifty-five. Still, the car behind them kept coming closer.

In a matter of moments, the lights were almost upon them, shining so brightly that they seemed to fill the whole wagon. Rob's passengers could barely stand to look, shielding their eyes with their arms.

"It's gonna hit us," exclaimed D.J. "Do something!"

But in that instant, even as the sound of D.J.'s voice resonated within Rob's car, the lights suddenly vanished.

Rob drove onward for moment, as his passengers sat in stunned silence. Then, as if awakening from a dream, Rob lifted his foot off the gas pedal and tapped the breaks, coasting to a stop. He looked at D.J. who sat panting beside him, clearly shaken by the encounter.

"What was that?" D.J. said, at last. He looked like he didn't want to hear the answer.

Rob shrugged. He shifted the car into park and climbed out. The others soon followed, even D.J. Together, they stared down the road behind them.

There was no sign of another car anywhere.

Interestingly enough, the encounter, as strange as it might have been, was not unique to Rob, D.J. and their friends. According to several accounts, it is one that repeated itself, time and again, over the course of several years. However, Denton Road Bridge is no longer what it used to be. It was replaced when the road was widened, and apparently the Denton Demon left with the old bridge. No encounters have been reported since.

A Gifted Child

"How much longer?" Julia whined from the backseat.

The drive up Interstate 75, from Cincinnati to Detroit, was a long one—especially for a six-year-old only child.

"We're almost home, honey," said her mother, Tonya Mindor. She had made the trip to Ohio with her daughter and husband just two days ago. It was a rare weekend visit to see Julia's grandparents. Now, as they neared the fourth hour of their trip back home to Detroit, Tonya remembered why these visits were such a rarity.

Still, it was nice to get away. Thanks to Julia's "gift," the house they lived in kind of gave Tonya the creeps.

In a lot of ways, Julia was a typical child. She loved to read books and to play with dolls. She dreamed of owning a pony. And she fought against baths and bedtime, tooth and nail. However, in one very distinct way, Julia was quite different from other children.

It was shortly after she turned three when the child first mentioned her paranormal acquaintance. "Mom," she had said. "There's a girl in my closet."

At first, Tonya and her husband assumed it was Julia's version of an imaginary friend. But the "friendship" quickly grew strange and macabre. Julia claimed her companion was a ghost, and as the relationship became darker and more intense, the Mindors began to wonder.

According to Julia, the ghost wore red and orange. It liked to play tricks and frighten her. The hallway and Julia's bedroom were the favored spots of the specter, whom the child claimed to see even when her parents could not.

There were times when Julia refused to walk down the hallway or to enter her bedroom. On other occasions, she might start toward her room, stop and hurry back, saying, "Nope. Ghost!"

Tonya, herself, had a couple of strange brushes with her daughter's ghostly guest.

"Julia, can you grab a shirt from your closet?" her mother asked, as she folded clothes in the living room.

"No way," replied her daughter, defiantly. "The ghost is there now."

"Don't be silly," said Tonya.

Julia crossed her arms and stomped her foot. "Mommy, I'm not going!"

Sensing the onset of a tantrum, Tonya quickly defused the situation. "I'll help you. Come with me." She led her daughter into the bedroom and flung open the closet door. "See? No ghost."

Tonya reached inside and picked out a shirt for Julia. "How's this one?"

The then four-year-old subtly nodded her approval. But she still looked scared, her face pale and her eyes turned away from the closet.

Tonya closed the door and started to say, "What's wrong?" But she stopped.

Knock. Knock.

The woman heard and felt two taps on the other side of the closet door. She quickly pulled it open again. No one was there, and everything was in place. Nothing had fallen against the door.

A few weeks later, Julia was again complaining about the mean-spirited spirit.

"Have you tried telling her to go away?" suggested Tonya, trying to hide the frustration in her voice. "Maybe if you tell her to leave you alone, she will."

Julia yelled toward the bathroom, "Go away. I don't want to play with you!"

Crash! An explosion of noise echoed from within the distant room.

Tonya hurried to investigate. She found Julia's mesh toy bag at the bottom of the bathtub. It had released itself from the shower wall, spilling its contents everywhere.

Yet another possible sign that Julia possessed a sixth sense was her fear of weeping willow trees. She said that she saw ghosts in them. At first, her parents thought it to be a bizarre claim. But later, they learned that some Native Americans believe spirits live in such trees. Julia's terror didn't seem so peculiar anymore.

Now, as the Mindors cruised up Interstate 75, on the outskirts of Detroit's metropolitan area, their daughter was about to surprise them again.

Two police cars screamed past the family, breaking the trip's monotony. The speeding vehicles stopped a few miles up the road. By the time the Mindors reached them, police officers were directing traffic off the freeway.

As the family neared the top of the ramp, Julia began to whimper. She curled into a ball and covered her eyes.

Tonya turned to check on her daughter. "What is it, honey? Why are you crying?"

Julia pointed out the window with one hand, shielding her eyes with the other. "There's a ghost lady on that bridge," the girl cried. "She's looking at me, and I don't want her to!"

"What does she look like?" asked Tonya.

"She's tall and skinny. She has dark hair, and she looks really sad."

Tonya immediately felt guilty for asking. Julia was clearly upset. The mother reached back and patted her daughter's arm, dropping the subject for good.

Later that night, safely at home and with their child sound asleep, Tonya and her husband tuned in for the local news. Their suspicions were confirmed. Earlier that day, on Interstate 75, near the spot where the Mindors had been rerouted, a tragic accident had occurred. While multiple cars and several people were involved, there was just one fatality: a tall, thin, dark-haired young woman.

Great Lake Ghosts

Minnie Quay

Brett Jordan had more than a passing fascination with ghosts and with haunted locales. He fancied himself as something of a ghost hunter (although he'd never had an actual encounter), and he knew the story of Minnie Quay well. So when he realized his business trip to Port Huron would bring him within 40 miles of Forester, he decided to plan a detour.

Thus, the twenty-six-year-old stood before one of the eastern coastal town's old, abandoned homes. "Quay, 1852," which was written above the door, signaled he had found the right place.

The house had once belonged to James and Mary Ann Quay, who moved to the area from New England. Neither could have guessed what the busy port town had in store for their daughter, Minnie.

With countless sailors traveling in and out of the area, many of Forester's young women fell for hard-working, fearless seafarers. Minnie Quay was no different. In 1876, at the age of fifteen, she met the love of her life.

James and Mary Ann disapproved of the blossoming relationship. Eventually, they forbade their daughter from seeing the sailor. Heartbroken, Minnie never got a chance to say goodbye to her beloved. He sailed out of Forester—for the final time.

In April, the teenaged girl received word that her seaman had died; his ship had sunk during a terrible Lake Huron storm. Minnie was devastated; she committed suicide, leaping off the pier into the same frigid waters that had claimed the life of her one true love.

Ever since that fateful day more than 130 years ago, a number of witnesses claimed to have seen Minnie's spirit wandering along the shores of Lake Huron. Brett hoped to spy her ghost, but he didn't truly believe he would.

"Are you another of them ghost chasers?" a young woman said suddenly.

Brett jumped, startled by the person he hadn't seen coming. He quickly gathered himself. "Sort of," he replied. Then he reconsidered. "Not really."

The thin, blonde girl who appeared to be nineteen or twenty didn't look at him. Instead, she stared straight ahead, speaking in a hollow, monotone voice. "It's real, you know: her ghost. I've seen it."

Brett wanted to answer, but the right words escaped him. He couldn't guess what a proper response would be.

His visitor continued. "I was walking near the lake. The sun was setting, and I saw a girl out there, in the water. It was cold; it's always so cold. I figured she must be drowning. But she wasn't. She was waving, telling me to come in—*begging* me to come in. It was weird too because, all of a sudden, I really wanted to. It didn't make sense, but I felt like I needed to be with her."

Brett stared, his mouth agape, waiting for the girl to continue. When she didn't, he asked, "What did you do?"

She didn't answer. Instead, she turned and looked at him, meeting his gaze for the first time. Then, in that instant, she faded away, evaporating like a cloud of mist.

Brett yelped. He stumbled backward before scurrying to his car. He hopped inside, locked the doors and sped away as quickly as the vehicle would accelerate.

Ghost Ship

The schooner was cursed. Of that, its crew seemed certain. In 1883, the *Erie Board of Trade* reached port on its way from Buffalo to Chicago, and one of its sailors shared a frightful story.

"It was the captain's fault," declared the crew member. "The boatswain's chair he gave Scotty wasn't safe. The rope was worn, and we all knew it. It was a death sentence to put anyone in it, but the captain didn't like Scotty."

"Why not?" a patron interrupted.

"Who knows? But the captain, he ignored the warnings. He sent that Scotsman up the rigging to scrape down the topmast. The poor kid didn't last a minute. The instant he put his weight in that chair, the rope snapped; he crashed to the deck."

There was an audible gasp amongst the listeners.

The storyteller continued. "The fall killed Scotty, but before it did, he whispered a curse against the captain and against the ship."

Many of the other sailors nodded their agreement. A few of them stood and hurried out of the tavern. They apparently did not want to hear the rest.

"We saw him die," the crewman added. "We witnessed it with our own eyes. But ever since, the thing of it is, some of us have seen Scotty wandering about the ship. His ghost is back to haunt us!"

Suddenly, the old man broke down, overwhelmed by emotion. He buried his face in his hands, and he sobbed. When at last he looked up, his eyes were wild with fear.

"I don't want to do it," the sailor spat. "I don't want to get back on that ship. It's cursed, I tell you. It's cursed!"

Shortly thereafter, the *Erie Board of Trade* departed. Within two days, it mysteriously sank in the icy waters of Lake Huron, killing everyone aboard.

Whether or not the old storyteller returned to the schooner, whether or not he died with the rest of the crew remains unknown. However, he—like the other brave souls aboard the *Erie Board of Trade*—was never seen again.

Just as it was for Scotty, death could not keep this ship down. The schooner can still be spotted, on occasion, a ghost ship sailing in Saginaw Bay.

Shrieks in the Stairwell

Laura Thomas loved lighthouses. In fact, her home's three-season porch was decorated with a lighthouse theme, its blue walls and white trim complemented by a variety of paintings, photographs and trinkets. Laura also enjoyed ghost stories. She collected spooky lighthouse tales like some people collect stamps.

Of course, there was the yarn about the Saginaw River Rear Range Light, north of Bay City. As the story went, an elderly lighthouse keeper on his deathbed asked his family to maintain the burning light. However, not trusting them to the task, the man's spirit remained and was often heard stomping up and down the stairs.

Another of her favorites involved a similar story at the lighthouse on Thunder Bay Island. There, too, the ghost of a former keeper was said to roam the lighthouse—and the entire island.

Laura enjoyed the scary tales, but she believed them to be just that: tales. Her perspective changed when she and her friend Angie toured the old Presque Isle Lighthouse in northeastern Michigan.

"This place has a tragic history," said Angie.

"Don't they all?" replied Laura with a shrug.

Angie continued. "Years ago, an old keeper had a wife, and they lived here alone, day after day. It was lonely for both of them—so much so that the isolation drove the poor woman insane. The keeper had to lock her away in here."

Laura shook her head. "That's terrible."

"I know," said Angie. "Worst of all, the poor woman eventually died in this place."

After a brief pause, Laura noted, "I suppose this light-house is haunted too." She was intrigued, although she couldn't help but wonder how much of Angie's account was true and how much was exaggeration.

As she climbed the stairs, her doubts were quickly dispelled. The lighthouse suddenly became filled with the sound of mad, horrifying screams.

The ghastly cries caused Laura's blood to run cold. She whispered rhetorically, "Do you hear that?" Then she gaped at her friend, whose face looked as pale as Laura's felt.

The shrieks grew louder, leaving her frozen with panic. For a long moment, Laura contemplated whether to find a place to hide or to investigate the noise.

Angie decided for both of them. She hurried down the steps; Laura instinctively followed.

As she rushed downward, Laura found herself half hoping to bear witness to some gruesome accident at the bottom of the stairwell. At least it would explain the awful pleas. The alternative was almost incomprehensible.

Yet to Laura's continued horror, she and Angie did not encounter another living soul. The screams seemed to come from everywhere and nowhere all at once.

Then, just as the women touched the outside door, the

piercing cries instantly ceased. The lighthouse was once again silent.

This sudden stillness was perhaps more unsettling than the screams had been. Laura hurried out the door and led Angie to her car. As they sped away, Laura couldn't help but think that the other lighthouse tales didn't seem so far-fetched anymore.

The Keeper's Ghost

Lonna Moore couldn't get the story out of her head. She loved hearing ghostly yarns by day, and the owners of the Big Bay Point Lighthouse Bed and Breakfast were more than happy to oblige. But now, as she lay awake in her dark accommodations, beside her snoring husband, she wished she hadn't indulged herself.

Reportedly, the old lighthouse was haunted by the spirit of its first keeper, William Prior. The man had started tending to the lighthouse in 1896, the year it was built. But tragically, his only son died a short while later. The lighthouse keeper, overwhelmed with grief, took his own life by hanging himself in the nearby woods. His spirit was said to reside within the restored Big Bay Point Light, which guarded the rugged and dangerous Lake Superior shore, thirty miles northeast of Marquette.

As if that tale weren't frightening enough, Lonna and her husband had also visited the Lumberjack Tavern in Big Bay. A friendly, "up north" place, the old restaurant was perhaps best known for the 1951 murder on the premises, an event which later spawned the book (and subsequent film) *Anatomy of a Murder.*

Now, as Lonna listened to each minute tick by, she couldn't decide which scared her more, her belief in ghosts or the reality of cold-blooded murder.

Suddenly, Lonna's thoughts were interrupted. Outside the room, a loud scraping noise and the rhythmic sound of footsteps carried through the hallway.

The woman tried to convince herself that this was perfectly explainable: It was another guest—or perhaps even the owners.

Initially, she resisted the urge to stir her husband. However, when she began to hear random doors opening and closing, Lonna couldn't wait any longer.

"Harold, wake up," the red-headed woman whispered. She grabbed his shoulder and gently shook him.

Her husband mumbled, almost inaudibly, and rolled away from her. Lonna shook him again, harder this time.

"What?" he said, without looking.

"I hear something," his wife whispered. "I think it might be a ghost."

Harold began to say, "That's ridiculous," and, "Those were just made-up stories." But he stopped. Or rather, he was interrupted—by a haunting moan.

Harold sat up. "What was that?"

Lonna nudged closer to him. "A ghost," she whispered.

"It can't be," replied the man.

The spirit of William Prior had the couple's attention, and it apparently had one more trick in store for them—one that would leave even Harold with little doubt about the ghostly presence.

As the husband and wife quietly debated whether there were or were not such things as ghosts, a light inside their room suddenly clicked on, all by itself.

It was a final, unexplainable act, contributing to a night at the Big Bay Point Lighthouse Bed and Breakfast that the Moores would never forget. The couple left the next day with a story they proudly shared for years to come.

A Deathly Dream

It was a terrible nightmare. Captain Truedell, an officer of the Great Lakes Lifesaving Service, had witnessed several tragic shipwrecks; his dream in August of 1892 seemed as real as any of them.

In his mind's eye, the captain saw a wealthy young man and his family aboard a steel-hulled freighter, cruising through Lake Superior's waters. The dreamer watched helplessly as the large ship broke in half and sank.

Nearly all of the freighter's thirty-two passengers and crew members managed to board one of two lifeboats, but the angry seas quickly overturned the first of them. Only two people survived the stormy waters long enough to join their companions on the remaining vessel.

By dawn, the occupants had rowed within a mile of shore. But just as they drew closer to safety, their boat too was swallowed by the sea.

Truedell awakened from his disturbing vision with a start. He should've felt relieved to learn that the harrowing ordeal was only a nightmare. Instead, he was shaken and disturbed; he sensed that he had experienced more than a simple bad dream.

On August 30, the famous financier Peter Minch sailed aboard a freighter, the *Western Reserve*, with his wife and two children. The steamer was on its way to pick up a load of ore in Two Harbors, Minnesota, when Truedell's dream became reality. Caught in a ferocious storm, Minch's ship broke in half and sank. Of the thirty-two passengers, only the wheelsman Harry Stewart survived.

Minch's body was among the few that were recovered. It washed up along shore near Deer Park. In a surprising coincidence, Truedell was reportedly the person who found it. The captain recognized the body immediately from the details of his dream.

As if that weren't bizarre enough, the *Western Reserve* continues to live in infamy. It is among the many ghost ships said to sail for all eternity in the waters that border the Great Lake State.

Selected Bibliography

American Hauntings. www.prairieghosts.com.
Troy Taylor. 2009.

Beast of Bray Road, The. Linda S. Godfrey. Prairie Oak
Press, Madison, WI. 2003.

Bowers Harbor Inn. www.bowersharborinn.net.

Haunted Heartland. Beth Scott and Michael Norman.
Barnes & Noble Books, New York. 1985.

Haunts of Mackinac. Todd Clements. House of Hawthorne
Publishing, Grosse Pointe, MI. 2006.

*Haunted Places: The National Directory: Ghostly Abodes,
Sacred Sites, UFO Landings and Other Supernatural
Locations.* Dennis William Hauck. Penguin Books,
New York. 2002.

Legend of the Michigan Dogman, The.
www.michigan-dogman.com.
Mindstage Productions. 2010.

Michigan's Otherside. www.michigansotherside.com. 2010.

Shadowlands, The. http://theshadowlands.net.
Dave Juliano. 2009.

Weird Michigan. Linda S. Godfrey, Mark Moran and Mark
Sceurman. Sterling Publishing, New York. 2006.

Upper Peninsula Paranormal Research Society.
www.upprs.org. Tim Ellis. 2009.

Index of Cities

About the Author

Nearly twenty years ago, Ryan Jacobson had a brush with the "unexplainable." Not long after, his older brother, Jason, introduced Ryan to his first horror novel. It was then that Ryan's love of reading ghost stories was born.

He later turned his passion for books into a career as an author, most recently focusing on "safe scary books for kids." He has written nine children's books, including a picture book, *Joe Lee and the Boo: Who's Afraid of Monsters?*, and a choose-your-path book, *Lost in the Wild*. Ryan also writes a web comic, *Monster Ninjas*™, and he is the author of *Ghostly Tales of Wisconsin*.

Ryan resides in Mora, Minnesota, with his wife, Lora, son, Jonah, and dog, Boo. For more about the author or to read his own ghostly tale, visit RyanJacobsonOnline.com.